THE PLEASURE STEAMERS

ANDREW MOTION

The Pleasure Steamers

CARCANET

Acknowledgements:

Acknowledgements are due to the editors of the following publications, in which these poems have appeared: *Agenda; Delta; Outposts; Poetry Book Society Supplement* (Christmas 1977); *PN Review; Stand; The Honest Ulsterman; The Listener; The New Review; Times Literary Supplement.*

'Inland' won the Newdigate Poetry Prize in 1975 and was published by the Cygnet Press (Burford, Oxford). 'The Pleasure Steamers' was published by the Sycamore Press (Oxford). 'Leaving Belfast' was one of the winners of the Cheltenham Festival Poetry Competition in 1977. A number of the poems were included in a collection which was given a Gregory Award in 1976.

First published in 1978
This impression 1999 by
Carcanet Press Limited
4th Floor, Conavon Court
12–16 Blackfriars Street
Manchester M3 5BQ

ISBN 0 85635 247 0

The publisher acknowledges financial assistance from
the Arts Council of England

Printed and bound in England by SRP Ltd, Exeter

FOR JOANNA JANE

CONTENTS

PART ONE

LETTER TO AN EXILE

I.

Today your letter with its usual banter of strangeness
—the forty years exile makes you write
'Napoli' now, without joking—until the postscript
'What would you say? Shall I come back?'

Was that unhurried? Or did you catch sight
over the quilted roofs of the steamer
returning here again? I know how it looks;
the rails freckled with figures who see

their wake scrawl itself out, and then,
beyond it, the hills reduced to mist
where they made their journeys, holidays,
abandoned attempts at a life.

These original, northern gravities!
Though it gave nothing, now England
renews its wide promises —the map,
hung in your room for sentiment,

daily becoming a landscape perfected
by absence; a locked island where riddles
abruptly solve; a spoor of rock
poised before the Atlantic.

II

Tonight I've come, as every night,
back to this lamp's blond pool, and here
is your letter again, weighed down,
repeating questions I cannot answer.

Other lamps hang in the city
through my window, changeable constellations,
lighting only the sleepless now,
the lonely listening for footsteps.

You say it was like that for you,
but you had visible danger —Spain waiting,
Europe waiting —and we have no sirens,
no wars, only a private, long progress

towards morning, without release
from what scarcely threatens us.
Look: their lights hold steady,
watching above the river; it uncoils

beyond my street, an oiled wire conducting
moonlight through derelict wharves,
and striking a swan's black foot,
arched underwater, swimming east.

III.

But you know about water, how it assures us
of elsewhere —and if I could, I'd say
come here, and the river will fill
your return with chances. But time,

which you think heals, has broken
that promise. Now where the current
slides under bridges, it only brings
scraps from inland—boughs without leaves,

planks, grass, representative lives
dragged down as if England was emptied
by water. Here silence is not the silence
you want, to hear wheat stirred through

remembered fields, or a bird calling
from childhood, but the same, deliberate
ignorance, peering at history for comfort,
you left to escape; it's concealed,

but it's always here, even now,
as early risers whistle up side streets,
and others above them stumble through
curtained rooms, into first light.

FOUNDATIONS

This summer the sun shone
hard for the new hotel:
wind that kept clouds high
overhead, dried scrubland
powdery on top as pepper
where digging began.

But now they are twenty feet
down, and the obdurate clay
holds them fast, sucking
spades, shoes, anything,
barrows even, deep under
its own thick territory.

All month I've seen men
tunnel themselves in like
—its first discoverers
I was going to say, except
that today a group suddenly
stood back pointing where

relics of two fish lay
coiled in rock, salmon,
which swam this field
before its clay came there,
or anyone ever looked down
through the immense air.

THE COLOUR WORKS

Ochre, really, but buried. To them it was just
'the colour', and tanned them yellow, as if
these vaults in the hill were journeys towards the sun.
Down there in the valley you'll see the rail
that ran it to Bristol; thin, adulterate stuff,
but how else could they have lived, with flints
for grazing, and towns a day's travel away?

Of course, it's different now;
after this road was built, the hill
returned to nothing but mud and simple stone.
Merely coincidence, but in a year the village
became an oddity, something to photograph:
groups in beards and shovel-shaped hats,
each of them stained an original sepia.

Still, the exhausted country they left
restores them; even today you stumble
on chains tangled in elder. The workings
have long since vanished in grass,
but no one who tosses a stone along
their dangerous corridors ever mistakes
the fall as a well, or sees it end.

What were the old days for, if not
exchanging the dark for legends?
Everyone knows it's wind underground
when slopes are howling in winter
—earth is earth, and all that survives
is rumour you've heard before. But look
at the swallows leaving that entrance there;
why do their wings beat out the colour of gold?

WISTMAN'S WOOD

for J. A. T. L.

We had gone to find trees,
but it is stones I remember first—
boulders of green granite forcing
roots above ground, turning every
strong wind back into Dartmoor.

They will survive the trees;
but not yet. Even midwinter
found orange buds risen already
through ten centuries' weather
into that gaunt spring for us.

'Listen', you said, 'Nothing at all.'
And nothing was all there was,
just twilight, casting us out
of ourselves and into the shadows,
into the fixed stones frozen over.

Did we think it could stay?
When I look back I see trees
hunched in the stillness,
and us ignoring whatever
might come, recalling only the lives

we'd left beyond our reach,
as far and faint that night
as now the stones are, where
we turned downhill at last
to home, towards the city lights.

INSIDE AND OUT

Two hundred miles from home I found
the one lonely room where you live,
and that, as you said, was 'Nothing,
really. Not even my own. See this?
It's Madame Dussart's funeral gown,
filling a whole drawer. Supposing
I died first, of boredom, what then?'

Then nothing again. A vacant room
where no one would see the sunlight
mark time in dust towards your bed.
As if we were ghosts of ourselves
we waited for darkness, watching it
deepen to bring us together again
like shadows, our close definition.

And shadows we stayed, or tried to,
knowing, before it fell, that night
after night would discover us still
caught in our absolute lives. If not
the room, what was there outside to blame,
hidden except when headlights below
reminded us where they travelled towards?

Vimy, Arras, Bapaume: I imagined
the brilliant signs, whitening south
through your country of maps and towns
in history. Nothing escaped itself—
not even the wind, tracing a ridge
of lost lines over the fields, always
raising the same delicate spray of graves.

They were complete societies, flickering
stones I knew by distant village names.
However I chose I remembered them,
all preserved no matter what deaths
succeeded them there, and us, who talking
each other to sleep at last heard only
their luminous silence we could not survive.

PAST MIDNIGHT

Past midnight now, I look down
from an open window: mist rides
on the river, and streets away
the lights of late travellers
circle, then turn into darkness.

They are all that remain of home,
these familiar signs—although
they explain and confirm nothing,
since they depend on you, and you
ignore them by seeming to sleep.

Your breathing steadies behind me,
drawn in where soon we shall lie
in silence again, not touching,
with only the moon to show us
the lives we found, and cannot keep.

LEAVING BELFAST

for Craig Raine

Driving at dusk on the steep road
north to the airport, 'Look back',
you say, 'The finest view of Belfast',
and point, proud of your choice to stay.

How clear the rows of streetlamps show
which way we came. I trace them slope
by slope through marshlands slipping down
to lanes, and find the roofs again,

their stern geographies of punishment
and love where silence deepens under rain.
Each sudden gust of light explains itself
as flames, but neither they, nor even

bombs redoubled on the hills tonight
can quite include me in their fear.
What does remains invisible, is lost
in curt societies whose deaths become

revenge by morning, and whose homes
are nothing more than all they pity most.
I watch the moon above them, filling rooms
with shadow politics, though whether

voices there pronounce me an intruder,
traitor, or a friend, I leave them now
as much a stranger as I came, and turn
to listen in the twilight for their griefs,

but hear instead the promise of conclusion
fading fast towards me through these miles
of stubborn gorse, until it disappears
at last in darkness, out beyond the coast.

LOOKING BACK

There were floods, I remember,
our final spring in the place,
and the week we left, the last
elms in the park were felled.

Between the wharves and two
steamers moored for winter
the blue foresters' lorry
drove through drowned levels,

floating logs towards the fire.
That was all I could see. But now,
living half the world and a year
away, I still imagine it there—

reflected flames, and smoke
rusting the first few cups
of yellow crocuses, and us
defined by warm, particular dust.

THE PLEASURE STEAMERS

I.

It's blowing cold from the east,
but still, they're working tonight
on the steamers, more shadows than men:
each canvas peels back like a chrysalis,

benches are turned to the view
in dusty saloons. It's as if I was
watching last summer restored. Or more
than last summer. The name picked out

in lights from the bridge is one
my father saw, lying offshore
in 1940, from France—*Mapledurham*
dark red for safety, and home.

Soon I'll take his place.
And though I've no danger
of dying, having no cause,
I'll look from the varnished deck

like him, not searching
for what I expect, but what I need:
cities reduced to innocent wharves; punts
moored over their image in obsolete pastoral.

II.

The river repeats itself, and I
repeat myself watching it; here is
my hand on the bridge as it was
this morning, and here in a crevice

of moss the match I dropped then.
Everything waits for me till I live
far enough forward to find it changed:
now what I see in the twilight

as logs, rotate on the current
as sluggish and matted as what
I guessed must have been hidden
early today. There was a van

drawn up by the rushes, and on the mud
a diver, easing his mask off,
calling 'I couldn't see anything'.
Neither could I. Just clouds

on indolent stretches of water,
and somewhere beneath it
an absence of light, increasing,
swelling towards me like rain.

24

III.

The steamers are ready:
one by one their lights go
out in the water, and in a day
they'll take up summer stations.

How can I help but admire
their implacable constancy?
Year after year I see them
leaving like gaudy ghosts

with nowhere to haunt
but their past. Defeats
and drownings have never
prevented their journey,

and now they're caught
in a separate world, sailing
for ever from here to the end
of a lost, inexhaustible century

where I may sometimes visit
but never stay, although
I discover at every return
I could have outlived myself there.

ANYWHERE BUT HERE

Now you are travelling back
to the place you love,
there's nothing here we can share
but time—and over us both
that full moon riding
in clear miles of migrating air.

Everything else goes with you;
even the lamps outside
drown in the river like rain,
and further, the park is invisible
that I must cross each day,
but never with you again.

Tomorrow others will take
the places we took to rest
your lovely head in my lap
—and in a day the city
will be an original strangeness,
herringbone lines on a map.

So look up, love, tonight:
an identical light will fall
on your tired, upturned face
as falls on mine. Whatever
traces remain of you here
survive independent of place.

NO NEWS FROM THE OLD COUNTRY

I.

Well, how do they look, the hills of Vermont,
now that you're back? Smaller? And closer the house?
In thirty years it isn't the weather that's changed them,
but you, contracting the past by turning away.

Restore it now. England's dependable winters
were never enough, but there, watching the hills
repeat their promise of danger, you're home
on original ground. Let it build back—

fresh shadows have pressed across your room,
and further, the forest you never explored
has flooded new valleys. O let it build back,
not as explicable, thin enchantment,

but as a place in extremity: all its rivers
and broken roads defining a wilderness
where you relearn your love of chances,
and, as I write, even by pushing out

through your gate towards the trees
to search for kindling, are suddenly lost
from sight in a flutter of snow from a bough,
and found in the dark, risking another world.

II.

So it goes on; so I, in the old country,
live off borrowed adventures. Since you left here
nothing has changed to disturb its complacent stillness;
or rather, there's only your absence starting again

each day, unreal and substantial at once,
like a hole in the air. But otherwise
there are the same identical views, which never
develop or move: the park, the thicket of steeples,

and even the river which carries down news
from miles inland is frozen across.
The rubbish of summer sealed in ice!
So much for different worlds. Where are you now?

High up in the woods, alone? Here there's only
the city's floodlit, familiar dark
fading towards you as England turns out of the sun.
O love, how did it start, this suburban safety,

this living on rumours of action? And now,
when will it end, pretending a possible happiness
somewhere else, another beginning, a river
tapped at its first, immaculate source?

28

OVER THE HILLS

When I look up
I expect to see the hills.
Today, across ten miles
of light, mist leaves them
clear; an ambushing, high crest
of stone, suspended for ever.

Your car dislodges
a few shadows. The hills stir
then settle between us again;
here what I call my own
is merely part of their legend,
when I say 'love'
it is overtaken by echoes.

Turning downhill, you go
south from their stiff swell.
I imagine it all:
the hills reduced to a thin
cinder of sunlight, your head
dragging free from their other lives.

HOMECOMING

Midnight; the station doors swing
shut, and here I am, walking
the frozen embankment home again.

Lights from the empty train
fall in flakes on the Thames,
showing a branch there, locked

in ice, and then in the gravel
footprints I made this morning,
still setting out. How long

must I travel to lose them?
Nowhere I've been today
has asked for anything

other than silence,
and no one I've seen
expected more from a stranger.

But now I come back to find
myself waiting to greet me,
bringing my name, and with it

the same unfinished ambitions,
the habits I cannot escape,
and even revive tonight

by stopping like this, to see
how frost tightens the delicate
rigging of trees I know,

and maps the river I hear
flowing ahead, concealed
under its flat quilt of snow.

PART TWO

32

INLAND

For Neil Rhodes

THE FENS and marshes of Cambridgeshire taper inland from the Wash almost to Cambridge itself. Although always vulnerable to any change in the water-table, the villagers in this area had learnt to respond to the fickleness of their environment by the end of the Middle Ages, and established common arable and grazing lands on which they could live with relative security.

In the early seventeenth century a fresh hazard arose. Commercially-minded lords and gentlemen assumed control of certain villages, claiming to be their landlords, and broke established social patterns by introducing enclosures. In coastal villages, where flooding was particularly severe, since high winter tides combined with the rise of fenland water, the intruders occasionally forced the villagers to abandon their homes and move to higher ground away from the more immediate danger. Unless support could be gained from a higher authority, local opposition to these schemes was vain.

The speaker of this poem is a member of such a village.

PART ONE: WINTER 1618

Evensong

'Christ is *your* King.' Jesse Sease, the preacher,
    says that, lifting one hand
and flooding our narrow church with shadow:
    'He gave you this land.'

I watch his shadows, trying to enter their darkness;
    they flicker on stone, then pass
over rows of sloped necks into the stiff folds
    of saints strolling in glass.

There is no comfort here, only a long absence
    where I exercise rage;
the real King is nearer, last night
    his men harassed the village,

mapping our fresh springs, describing our fields
    with their lamps.
Soon they will come again; already perspectives
    shift under the stamp

of their will. Until then, as I look up,
    the place returns to me:
God's unfinished landscape, an empty marsh, the sun
    dissolving light in the North Sea.

A View from the Porch

I grew up here, I know
how to possess the place;
its watery secrets, its slow
gestation of sinuous roots
will go if I go.

We built this wall to keep
tides from it. We thought life
transferred from hands to the steep
rim of our world would define
our claim, secure us the easy sleep

of rightful inheritors. But still
the tides come in, slithering
over the wall each winter until
they cancel our ditches, drown
the crops on our low hills.

Under their swell, the wall's strong
unbroken wake always survives;
now I will imitate where I belong
—that white arm lining the bay
limits the hope I live among.

Walking Home

Someone is playing a flute as I walk home
    by the wall; the notes
tauten on miles of blue, feathery marsh, then break
    across estuaries, boats,

and into the flat sea. Hung round the bay
    houses look down to it,
occasional bleached walls twisting a lamplight
    out through a slit,

most abandoned. The notes repeat and repeat
    over smashed beams,
a drift of tinkling dust, rephrasing
    their dispossessed dreams.

So many have left already, their rooms
    darkened again
by strangers completing the King's command:
    what remains

is only their echo returning to silence,
    and us, lingering here
ensnared by memory; pride;
    fear.

Home

Wind shakes the door.
Love, kneel by me here
at the fire, before
its warmth fails. Darkness
has smothered the sea's roar,

and even the strangers
sleep in their rough camps;
now while the globe blurs,
take my life in your hands
out of all danger.

Shadow falls from your face
into the red flames; let it
lie there, until each trace
of the present burns, and we
are without place.

Tomorrow, high tides will press
our future from us
back into emptiness;
so now, unpin your hair,
open your dress.

High Tide

A bar of moonlight tilts beyond the head,
melts underwater, then hauls in
the tide towards us on a liquid thread.
Early ripples smear against the wall.

Out there, the sea
reflects its planet's flawless steps,
—element with element in sympathy
obliterating margins round the bay.

The marsh contracts beneath their weight,
its channels reeled uphill
as hour by hour the breakers grate
closer through deserted lanes

until the farmlights gleam like ships
and running shadows wash across our room.
Look: below the window, contours slip,
unravelled between waves and light;

a gauze of slime has trailed above
the low wall at the estuary,
and fields must open to the water's shove,
where fish already strain inland.

PART TWO: WINTER 1618—SPRING 1619

Arrival

They came before dawn. Eddon, our neighbour, woke us,
    his boots splashed through
the yard, dragging a dark trail to our room:
    'Come quick. They want you.'

The darkness bared its miracle, slowly.
    We stood leaning our hands
on the window, watching below us a gull
    slide into fluid land,

then farms marooned on their ridge, flash open
    shutters, and lights
jog up a lane, halting where water
    gleamed out of sight

to its distant sea. For miles inland
    a few hills, sluggish
and crested from froth, heaved up
    their crowns like fish.

'Quick. They want you.' I thought he meant flooding.
    When I turned back
I saw the strangers' boat ploughing the marsh,
    and grass foam in their track.

Disembarkation

Sun flicked round the bay,
binding the outline of farms
to their reflections in grey
bands of light. The marsh
always survives. Always.

Cattle bunched in their shed,
uncoiling sweet wisps
of breath over my head;
fresh shadows spilt down
their flanks and spread

across water to flake
into shrinking fragments
over the strangers' wake.
Their boat put down
some men; one staked

its prow into our land,
waded towards us
over the grass, and
lifted one arm. Our world
dried on his hand.

An Ultimatum

I waited in silence, weighing a stone in my pocket,
    on our green beach;
a low boat swerved from the other's shadow
    and moored out of reach.

We saw nothing exactly; a stranger
    hunched in the stern
studied our silence, then stood. In the village
    behind us, quietly, locks turned.

Even his words were blurred by distance;
    we pressed to the shore,
thinking if this was the danger we feared,
    there must be more.

But as we stared at his elegant silhouette,
    into the sun,
we heard a tiny ripple of syllables claiming
    the village, then run

underwater over our fields until we were strangers
    in our own land,
watching our shadows circle on memories we could no
                  longer lose,
    or understand.

An Appeal Refused

In the church it was cold:
we knelt by the altar
waiting for fields to unfold
indoors the scent from flowers
of tamarisk, marsh marigold.

How could I leave that place?
I could imagine nothing except
its imperfect, stubborn grace
—but from the shadows
no saviour unveiled his face.

Did we want miracles? Signs?
I only saw light,
piercing the window, define
a forbidden landscape where
water and earth entwined.

We knelt until sunset burned
it to dark. Below us, as lamps
in the village returned,
out of the dark a thickening
silence smothered the love we earned.

Jesse Sease

Jesse Sease walked hunched, head weighed down
to take in the flat parish he lived for.
At noon on our last day, crossing the crown
of dry land, he stooped into his stone church

and knelt until evening, below his high shadow
hardening in the glass. When he came out
he walked to our yard: 'Go on up. I'll follow.'
One hand with its heavy ring picked at some cloth

on our cart; hens clucked through a dark door.
We could not meet his look, or anyone's,
but travelled inland towards our new law,
hoarding familiar, fragrant dust on boots and hair.

He must have stood by his church
watching our backs thinning in twilight,
then turned to the silver water, and lurched
in. We only heard our rough wheels grind uphill.

Searching next morning, we found him
drowned in the salty grass. He lay
with his head bending the water's rim,
the ring embedded in his swollen hand.

PART THREE: SUMMER 1619—WINTER 1619

In the New Village

This village disturbs the sky; white columns of air
    crumble over its stone,
and today we wake further into the deep hill
    we disown.

Eddon is crossing the street, pushing through
    heavy outlines of light
—look how the air shrinks him at once,
    restoring its right

to this place. Now murmuring heads turn
    behind walls,
hearing his stick tap down to the strangers' house,
    his thin call,

and his sacks bumped on their step.
    He will come back through
new fields, watching again their tight acres
    drain out of view:

a broad pan of gold poured up switching hedges
    until it joins
the hill's unnatural gravity, and sets
    in the strangers' hands, as coins.

Breaking Ground

Round the hill, grass
is churned into plough
where the horses pass,
until the village is hooped
with pliant, unravelling brass.

The share tosses and falls
in its own dilating swell,
dragging the men who crawl
in its shadow down to the dark
furrow they trawl.

I stand in the lane,
watching them curl round
the slope and appear again,
already wearing the sodden mud
knee-high, like a chain.

Past them, leaves are frayed
from the hedges; they twirl
overhead, then spray
out to sea, and vanish,
sudden and mute as days.

Visiting the Old House

Nothing conceals the hill, but from here
    the marshes insist
its distant curve is merely a band
    of rigid mist.

Here frost has settled like dust, stiffening grass
    and the trees
we planted as children, thinking to lie there
    at ease.

Last summer has sleeked their fruit, but snapped
    already the delicate hasps,
and in front of the house each skeletal bowl
    sizzles with wasps.

Remember the boughs that cocooned our room
    with shade?
Now through its windows their leaves spin
    in an airless cascade,

and when I look in, I see no trace
    of the trust we reached;
only, in darkness, abandoned chairs
    in a posture of speech.

A Last Look

Where I stand
the world centres on marshes
of black sand
—they are a wound, sunk
in the haunch of England.

No footprints now,
but pools in derelict
green ridges of plough,
where wind pulls voices
down from the hill-brow.

Marram in front of me
raises a tiny storm
as seeds blow free,
then breaks in a solid
wave against the whitening sea.

Now nothing survives
but tides wrestling with earth.
In the wake of our lives
weed fattens through dykes.
A drowned silence revives.

Leaving

Gulls veer overhead in splintered light;
'Storm' you say, watching their shadows
dodge down the lane. From that height
you would see on the hill behind us

men pause to look up, then drag stooks
through yellow fields into barns, still
moving in habits of land they forsook,
as if there was hope to protect.

Slipping clear of its sky, the gulls
vanish up shrinking rivers, west
into England. Behind them, a lull
opens between two worlds: we are

without past now, waiting for lights
to come on in foreign towns
and define the lane's hard, white
cord stretching inland, valleys

travelled with shadow turning
their moonlit slopes in our glance,
and your hands, caught in mid-air,
stretched towards promise of distance.

PART THREE

A DYING RACE

The less I visit, the more I think
myself back to your elegant house
I grew up in. The drive uncurled
through swaying chestnuts discovers
it standing four square, white-
washed unnaturally clear,
as if it were shown me by lightning.

It's always the place I see,
not you. You're somewhere outside,
waving goodbye where I left you
a decade ago. I've even lost sight
of losing you now; all I can find
are the mossy steps you stood on
—a visible loneliness.

I'm living four counties away, and still
I think of you driving south each night
to the ward where your wife
is living. How long will it last?
You've made that journey six years
already, taking comparative happinesses
like a present, to please her.

I can remember the fields you pass,
the derelict pill-boxes squatting
in shining plough. If I was still there,
watching your hand push back
the hair from her desperate face,
I might have discovered by now the way
love looks, its harrowing clarity.

IN THE ATTIC

Even though we know now
your clothes will never
be needed, we keep them,
upstairs in a locked trunk.

Sometimes I kneel there,
holding them, trying to relive
time you wore them, to remember
the actual shape of arm and wrist.

My hands push down between
hollow, invisible sleeves,
hesitate, then lift
patterns of memory:

a green holiday, a red christening,
all your unfinished lives
fading through dark summers,
entering my head as dust.

ANNIVERSARIES

The Fourth
Anniversary weather: I drive
under a raw sunset, the road
cramped between drifts, hedges
polished into sharp crests.

I have it by heart now;
on this day in each year
no signposts point anywhere
but east into Essex,

and so to your ward,
where snow recovers tonight
the ground I first saw lost
four winters ago.

Whatever time might bring,
all my journeys take me
back to this dazzling dark:
I watch my shadow ahead

plane across open fields,
out of my reach for ever,
but setting towards your bed
to find itself waiting there.

54

The First
What I remember is not
your leaving, but your not
coming back —and snow
creaking in thick trees,

burying tracks preserved
in spiky grass below.
All afternoon I watched
from the kitchen window

a tap thaw in the yard,
oozing into its stiff sack,
then harden when evening
closed with ice again.

And I am still there,
seeing your horse return
alone to the open stable,
its reins dragging behind

a trail across the plough,
a blurred riddle of scars
we could not decipher then,
and cannot heal now.

The Second
I had imagined it all—
your ward, your shaved head,
your crisp scab struck there
like an ornament,

but not your stillness.
Day after day I saw
my father leaning forward
to enter it, whispering

'If you can hear me now,
squeeze my hand', till snow
melted in sunlight outside
then turned to winter again

and found him waiting still,
hearing the slow hiss
of oxygen into your mask,
and always turning to say

'Yes, I felt it then',
as if repeating the lie
had gradually made it true
for him, never for you.

56

The Third
Three years without sight,
speech, gesture, only
the shadow of clouds
shifting across your face

then blown a world away.
What sleep was that, which
light could never break?
What spellbound country

claimed you, forbidding you
even to wake for a kiss?
If it was death,
whose hands were those

warm in my own, and whose
astonishing word was it
that day when leaving
your sunlit room I heard

'Stay; stay', and watched
your eyes flick open once,
look, refuse to recognize
my own, and turn away?

The Fourth
The evening falls with snow
beginning again, halving
the trees into whiteness,
driving me with it towards

the end of another year.
What will it send for you
that this has abandoned?
You are your own survivor,

bringing me back the world
I knew, without the time
we lost; until I forget
whatever it cannot provide

I'll always arrive like this,
having no death to mourn,
but rather the life we share
nowhere beyond your room,

our love repeating itself
like snow I watch tonight,
which spins against my window
then vanishes into the dark.

THE LEGACY

Ashes have scattered her,
her money disowns her,
but I sit down to write
at the desk she willed me,
watching the lamp resurrect
her glistening lives:

layer after layer I inherit
their light immortality,
where in the end my hand
will sign my furniture on
to children or friends,
before it stops still as hers,

and then is replaced again
in distant, unvisited rooms,
transcribing itself for ever
like shadows which follow it now,
uncurling themselves in silence
on printed paper and skin.